The Fixer's Lesson on: Screws

Level 5 – Green

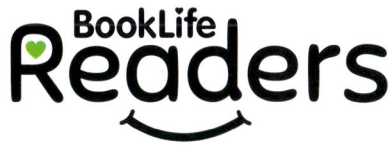

Helpful Hints for Reading at Home

The graphemes (written letters) and phonemes (units of sound) used throughout this series are aligned with Letters and Sounds. This offers a consistent approach to learning whether reading at home or in the classroom.

HERE IS A LIST OF NEW PHONEMES FOR THIS PHASE OF LEARNING. AN EXAMPLE OF THE PRONUNCIATION CAN BE FOUND IN BRACKETS.

Phase 5			
ay (day)	ou (out)	ie (tie)	ea (eat)
oy (boy)	ir (girl)	ue (blue)	aw (saw)
wh (when)	ph (photo)	ew (new)	oe (toe)
au (Paul)	a_e (make)	e_e (these)	i_e (like)
o_e (home)	u_e (rule)		

Phase 5 Alternative Pronunciations of Graphemes			
a (hat, what)	e (bed, she)	i (fin, find)	o (hot, so, other)
u (but, unit)	c (cat, cent)	g (got, giant)	ow (cow, blow)
ie (tied, field)	ea (eat, bread)	er (farmer, herb)	ch (chin, school, chef)
y (yes, by, very)	ou (out, shoulder, could, you)		

HERE ARE SOME WORDS WHICH YOUR CHILD MAY FIND TRICKY.

Phase 5 Tricky Words			
oh	their	people	Mr
Mrs	looked	called	asked
could			

TOP TIPS FOR HELPING YOUR CHILD TO READ:

- Allow children time to break down unfamiliar words into units of sound and then encourage children to string these sounds together to create the word.

- Encourage your child to point out any focus phonics when they are used.

- Read through the book more than once to grow confidence.

- Ask simple questions about the text to assess understanding.

- Encourage children to use illustrations as prompts.

This book focuses on the phoneme /ew/ and is a green level 5 book band.

How many words can you list with **ew** in?

Oh dear! Look at this mess. But this is the Fixer – he can fix it all! Phew!

He can fix it all with screws. Screws are long and thin, but they are not like nails.

Nails are hit into things with a hammer.
A drill twists a screw into an object.

Drill

The tip of the screw has a sharp point. This helps it to twist into an object.

Tip

There are a lot of screw tops. Some have got a cross and some do not.

Each turn of the screw will push it farther and farther into the object.

Screws can go into lots of things, such as wood and bricks.

A bolt is a sort of screw. It twists into an object called a nut. The nut keeps the bolt secure.

Some bolts can be big. They might need a big spanner to keep them tight.

Spanner

The Fixer has been fixing things with screws all day. Now they look new!

Not all screws are long and thin.
Which screws have you seen?

Taps are screws.

Lids can be screws.

Do not chew your pen lid. The lid might be a screw!

Some light bulbs have a screw.

©This edition published in 2023. First published in 2021.
BookLife Publishing Ltd.
King's Lynn, Norfolk PE30 4LS UK

ISBN 978-1-83927-903-4

All rights reserved. Printed in China.
A catalogue record for this book is
available from the British Library.

The Fixer's Lesson on: Screws
Written by William Anthony
Designed by Amy Li

An Introduction to BookLife Readers...

Our Readers have been specifically created in line with the London Institute of Education's approach to book banding and are phonetically decodable and ordered to support each phase of the Letters and Sounds document.

Each book has been created to provide the best possible reading and learning experience. Our aim is to share our love of books with children, providing both emerging readers and prolific page-turners with beautiful books that are guaranteed to provoke interest and learning, regardless of ability.

BOOK BAND GRADED using the Institute of Education's approach to levelling.

PHONETICALLY DECODABLE supporting each phase of Letters and Sounds.

EXERCISES AND QUESTIONS to offer reinforcement and to ascertain comprehension.

CLEAR DESIGN to inspire and provoke engagement, providing the reader with clear visual representations of each non-fiction topic.

AUTHOR INSIGHT:
WILLIAM ANTHONY

Despite his young age, William Anthony's involvement with children's education is quite extensive. He has written over 60 titles with BookLife Publishing so far, across a wide range of subjects. William graduated from Cardiff University with a 1st Class BA (Hons) in Journalism, Media and Culture, creating an app and a TV series, among other things, during his time there.

William Anthony has also produced work for the Prince's Trust, a charity created by HRH The Prince of Wales, that helps young people with their professional future. He has created animated videos for a children's education company that works closely with the charity.

PHASE 5 /ew/

This book focuses on the phoneme /ew/ and is a green level 5 book band.

Image Credits Images are courtesy of Shutterstock.com. With thanks to Getty Images, Thinkstock Photo and iStockphoto.
Cover – Amy Li, agolndr, Boonchuay1970, Anatolir, Nuttapong Photographer, p2–3 – Amy Li, Albo003, alisafarov, DONOT6_STUDIO, SomprasongWittayanupakorn, p4–5 – Tartila, Triff, p6–7 – AnotherPerfectDay, Perutskyi Petro, rafa jodar, p8–9 – Andrey Burmakin, Aryze, p10–11 – JIANG HONGYAN, Lena Ogurtsova, p12–13 – Nuttapong Photographer, Amy Li, thewada1976, p14–15 – AlenKadr, Chepko Danil Vitalevich, Sabina Leopa, Somchai Som.